CAT NAPS

First published in Great Britain in 2006 by
Michael O'Mara Books Limited
9 Lion Yard
Tremadoc Road
London SW4 7NQ

First published in the United States of America
in 2003 by Ronnie Sellers Productions, Inc.

A CIP catalogue record for this book is available from the British Library.

ISBN (13 digit): 978-1-84317-228-4
ISBN (10 digit): 1-84317-228-3

1 3 5 7 9 10 8 6 4 2

Series Editor: Robin Haywood
Photo Editor: Amanda Mooney
Designer: Patti Urban

Printed in China

CAT NAPS

Michael O'Mara Books Limited

Life is hard,
then you nap.

Anonymous

The idea of calm
exists in a sitting cat.

Jules Renard

There is more to life
than increasing its speed.

Mohandas Gandhi

8

If I didn't woke up,
I'd still be sleeping!

Yogi Berra

I don't know why it is we
are in such a hurry to get
up when we fall down.
You might think we would
lie there and rest a while.

Max Forrester Eastman

If there were to be
a universal sound
depicting peace,
I would surely vote
for the purr.

Barbara L. Diamond

The best cure
for insomnia is
to get a lot of sleep.

W.C. Fields

Light be the earth upon you, lightly rest.

Euripides

Learning to ignore
things is one of the
great paths to
inner peace.

Robert J. Sawyer

21

How beautiful it is to do nothing,
and then to rest afterward.

Spanish proverb

Champagne wishes
and caviar dreams . . .

Anonymous

Cats are rather delicate creatures
and they are subject to a good many
ailments, but I never heard of one
who suffered from insomnia.

Joseph Wood Krutch

26

A cat pours his
body on the
floor like water.
It is restful just
to see him.

William Lyon Phelps

I have never taken
any exercise except
sleeping and resting.

Mark Twain (Samuel L. Clemens)

Who among us hasn't envied a cat's ability to ignore the cares of daily life and to relax completely?

Karen Brademeyer

Take rest;
a field that has rested
gives a bountiful crop.

Ovid

The secret of happiness
is to make others believe
they are the cause of it.

Al Batt

Oh sleep! It is a gentle thing,
Beloved from pole to pole.

Samuel Taylor Coleridge

Slow down and enjoy life.
It's not only the scenery
you miss by going too fast
– you also miss the sense
of where you are going
and why.

Eddie Cantor

Sleep is the
best meditation.

Tenzin Gyatso,
the 14th Dalai Lama

There's never enough time to do all the nothing you want.

Bill Watterson,
Calvin and Hobbes

Loafing needs no explanation
and is its own excuse.

Christopher Morley

Yawn and the world
yawns with you.
Snore and you
sleep alone.

Anonymous

Nature does not
hurry, yet everything
is accomplished.

Lao-tzu

There is more
refreshment and
stimulation in a nap,
even of the briefest,
than in all the alcohol
ever distilled.

Edward Lucas

No day is so bad it can't
be fixed with a nap.

Carrie Snow

Dreams are only thoughts you didn't
have time to think about during the day.

Author unknown

Very little is needed
to make a happy life.

Marcus Aurelius Antoninus

Taking a nap,
feet planted
against a cool wall.

Matsuo Basho, 'Taking a Nap'

If there is one spot
of sun spilling on to
the floor, a cat will
find it and soak it up.

Jean Asper-McIntosh

It takes a lot of time
to be a genius, you
have to sit around so
much doing nothing,
really doing nothing.

Gertrude Stein

Slow down and everything you are chasing

will come around and catch you.

John DePaola

The fog comes
on little cat feet.

Carl Sandburg, 'The Fog'

Subliminal kitty messages?
'You are getting very sleepy'
is not a command when said
to a cat; it is an eternal truth.

Ari Ripkin

Follow your bliss and doors will open where there were no doors before.

Joseph Campbell

Kittens are born with their eyes shut. They open them in about six days, take a look around, then close them again for the better part of their lives.

Stephen Baker

The time to relax is when you don't have time for it.

Author unknown

BINOCULARS A FIELD GUIDE TO THE BUTTERFLIES OF *The East* BIRDS

There is a luxury in being
quiet in the heart of chaos.

Virginia Woolf

Everything I know
I learned from my cat:
When you're hungry, eat.
When you're tired,
nap in a sunbeam.
When you go to the vet's,
pee on your owner.

Gary Smith

There is no need to go to India or anywhere else to find peace. You will find that deep place of silence right in your room, your garden, or even your bathtub.

Dr. Elisabeth Kübler Ross, M.D.

A little drowsing cat is an image of perfect beatitude.

Jules Champfleury

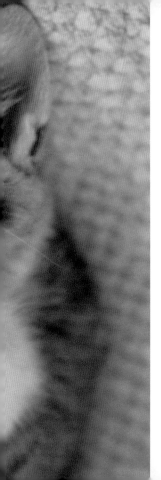

Don't underestimate
the value of doing nothing,
of just going along, listening
to all the things you can't hear,
and not bothering.

Pooh's Little Instruction Book

To sleep is
an act of faith.

Barbara G. Harrison

He seems the incarnation of everything soft and silky and velvety, without a sharp edge in his composition, a dreamer whose philosophy is sleep and let sleep.

Saki (H.H. Munro)

Now I see the secret of the making of the best persons. It is to grow in the open air and to eat and sleep with the earth.

Walt Whitman,
'Song of the Open Road'

It takes a lot of courage
to show your dreams
to someone else.

Erma Bombeck

Festina lente:

Make haste slowly.

Latin proverb

Prowling his own quiet backyard or asleep by the fire, he is still only a whisker away from the wilds.

Jean Burden

The future belongs to those who believe
in the beauty of their dreams.

Eleanor Roosevelt

Rest is not idleness,
and to lie sometimes
on the grass under a tree
on a summer's day,
listening to the murmur
of the water, or watching
the clouds float across
the sky, is by no means
a waste of time.

J. Lubbock

Which is more beautiful:
feline movement
or feline stillness?

Elizabeth Hamilton

A good laugh and
a long sleep are
the best cures in
the doctor's book.

Irish proverb

Cats are connoisseurs
of comfort.

James Herriot

Credits

Davies; pp. 80-81 photo © Hiroaki Shibata/A.collection/amana; pp. 82-83 © Ken Ross and Dr. Elisabeth Kübler Ross, M.D., from Real Taste of Life by Ken Ross and Dr. Elisabeth Kübler Ross, M.D., photo © Claudia Gorman; pp. 84-85 photo © Torahiko Yamashita/A.collection/amana; pp. 86-87 from Pooh's Little Instruction Book, inspired by A.A. Milne, published by Penguin Group USA/Dutton, photo © Torahiko Yamashita/A.collection/amana; pp. 88-89 photo © PhotoAlto/Creatas; pp. 90-91 photo © Neo Vision/Getty; pp. 92-93 photo © Koichiro Shimauchi/A.collection/amana; pp. 94-95 photo © Torahiko Yamashita/A.collection/amana; pp. 96-97 photo © Torahiko Yamashita/A.collection/amana; pp. 98-99 photo © Grace Davies; pp. 100-101 photo © Torahiko Yamashita/A.collection/amana; pp. 102-103 photo © Koichiro Shimauchi/A.collection/amana; pp. 104-105 photo © Torahiko Yamashita/A.collection/amana; pp. 106-107 photo © Torahiko Yamashita/A.collection/amana; pp. 108-109 photo © Koichiro Shimauchi/A.collection/amana.

101 Uses
for a
JACK
Russell

PHOTOGRAPHY BY DUŠAN SMETANA

WILLOW CREEK PRESS
MINOCQUA, WISCONSIN

Published by Willow Creek Press
P.O. Box 147 • Minocqua, Wisconsin 54548

Editor/Design: Andrea Donner

Library of Congress Cataloging-in-Publication Data
Smetana, Dusan.
   101 uses for a Jack Russell / photography by Dusan Smetana.
     p. cm.
   1. Jack Russell terrier--Pictorial works. 2. Photography of
dogs. I. Title: One hundred one uses for a Jack Russell. II.
Title: One hundred and one uses for a Jack Russell. III. Title.
   SF429.J27S64 2004
   636.755--dc22

2004019041

Printed in Canada

JACK RUSSELLS

In and Around the House

Uses 1-26

1

Dishwasher

2

Garbage disposal

3

Vice grips

4

Weed killer

5

Bookends

6

Boot warmer

7

Foot stool

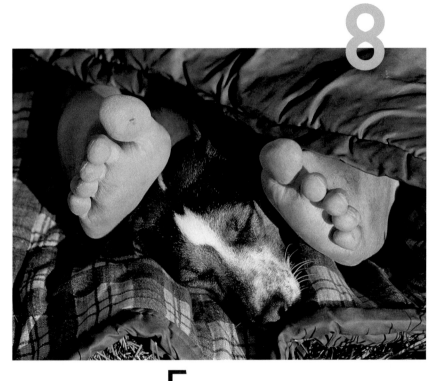

8

Foot warmer

9

Luggage

Garden gnome

11

Baby sitter

Cat sitter

13

Someone who takes you on a walk

14

Someone who laughs at your jokes

15

Welcome mat

101 Uses for a Jack Russell

Doorman

17

Pest control

101 USES FOR A JACK RUSSELL

Shovel

19

Car security system

Alarm bell

21

Security fence

22

Border patrol

23

Wash cloth

24

Toy

25

Hood ornament

101 USES FOR A JACK RUSSELL

Pillow

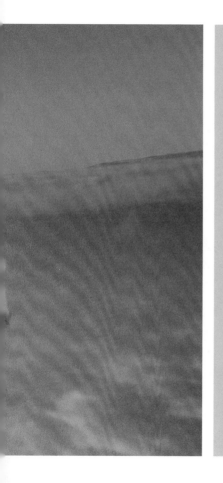

JACK RUSSELLS

As Athletes

Uses 27-56

Someone to play catch with

101 USES FOR A JACK RUSSELL

28

Acrobat

29

Dumbbells

Trail blazers

31

Street performer

Archer

33

Sprinters

34

Long-distance runner

35

Hurdler

36

All-Star wrestlers

37

Outfielders

38

Ball boy

39

Hiking buddy

Adventurer

Explorer

42

Rock climbers

43

Fishing pal

Hunting partner

44

45

Rafting guide

46

Mountain climber

47

Ski bum

Swimmer

49

Retriever

101 Uses for a Jack Russell

Lumberjack

51

Balancing Act

101 Uses for a Jack Russell

Competitor

53

$\int$lalom ace

101 USES FOR A JACK RUSSELL

54

Expert climber

55

Flats fisherman

B each comber

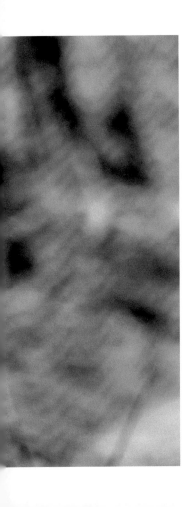

JACK RUSSELLS
Special Uses

Uses 57-101

Bike buddy

Biker buddy

Back-up singer

Snoop

61

Spy

Lookout

63

Someone who reminds you to
stop and smell the flowers …

64

... and roll in them sometimes too

65

Pack animal

66

Comedian

Vacation date

Beach bum

69

Trouble maker

Barrel full of fun

71

S now plow

101 USES FOR A JACK RUSSELL

Snow angel

73

A masseuse for when your neck is sore

A scarf for when your neck is cold

Someone to grow up with

101 Uses for a Jack Russell

Family members

77

Crowd pleasers

101 USES FOR A JACK RUSSELL

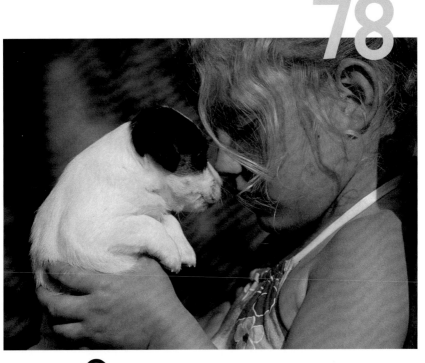

Someone to tell your secrets to

79

Sentry

First mate

Someone who's always got your back

Someone to have a picnic with

Postal inspector

Peace activist

Attentive listener ...

101 Uses for a Jack Russell

86

... sometimes

Co-pilot

Navigator

89

Someone to play hide-and-seek with

Farm hands

Fashion model

Fashion victims

Lap warmer

Smart aleck

Seat stealer

Heart stealer

Someone who gives hugs ...

... and kisses on demand

99

Someone who looks up to you...

... and is always happy to see you

101

Best friend